HAL LEONARD

UKULELE SONGS

T0080165

Ukulele by Chris Kringel

ISBN 978-1-4803-6817-0

HAL•LEONARD®
CORPORATION
7777 W. BLUEMOUND RD. P.O. BOX 13819 MILWAUKEE, WI 53213

Visit Hal Leonard Online at
www.halleonard.com

UKULELE NOTATION LEGEND

THE MUSICAL STAFF shows pitches and rhythms and is divided by bar lines into measures. Pitches are named after the first seven letters of the alphabet.

TABLATURE graphically represents the ukulele fingerboard. Each horizontal line represents a a string, and each number represents a fret.

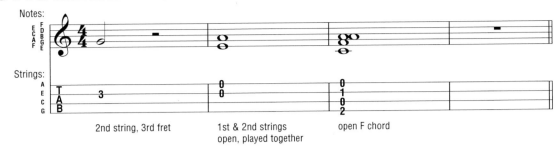

2nd string, 3rd fret | 1st & 2nd strings open, played together | open F chord

HALF-STEP BEND: Strike the note and bend up 1/2 step.

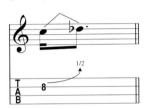

WHOLE-STEP BEND: Strike the note and bend up one step.

GRACE NOTE BEND: Strike the note and immediately bend up as indicated.

SLIGHT (MICROTONE) BEND: Strike the note and bend up 1/4 step.

BEND AND RELEASE: Strike the note and bend up as indicated, then release back to the original note. Only the first note is struck.

PRE-BEND: Bend the note as indicated, then strike it.

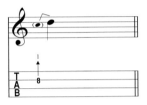

VIBRATO: The string is vibrated by rapidly bending and releasing the note with the fretting hand.

HAMMER-ON: Strike the first (lower) note with one finger, then sound the higher note (on the same string) with another finger by fretting it without picking.

PULL-OFF: Place both fingers on the notes to be sounded. Strike the first note and without picking, pull the finger off to sound the second (lower) note.

LEGATO SLIDE: Strike the first note and then slide the same fret-hand finger up or down to the second note. The second note is not struck.

SHIFT SLIDE: Same as legato slide, except the second note is struck.

TRILL: Very rapidly alternate between the notes indicated by continuously hammering on and pulling off.

TREMOLO PICKING: The note is picked as rapidly and continuously as possible.

NOTE: Tablature numbers in parentheses mean:

1. The note is being sustained over a system (note in standard notation is tied), or

2. The note is sustained, but a new articulation (such as a hammer-on, pull-off, slide or vibrato) begins, or

3. The note is a barely audible "ghost" note (note in standard notation is also in parentheses).

Additional Musical Definitions

 (accent) • Accentuate note (play it louder)

 (staccato) • Play the note short

D.S. al Coda • Go back to the sign (𝄋), then play until the measure marked "*To Coda*," then skip to the section labelled "**Coda**."

D.C. al Fine • Go back to the beginning of the song and play until the measure marked "*Fine*" (end).

N.C. • No chord.

 • Repeat measures between signs.

| 1. | 2. | • When a repeated section has different endings, play the first ending only the first time and the second ending only the second time.

UKULELE SONGS

Daughter

Words and Music by Stone Gossard, Jeffrey Ament, Eddie Vedder, Michael McCready and David Abbruzzese

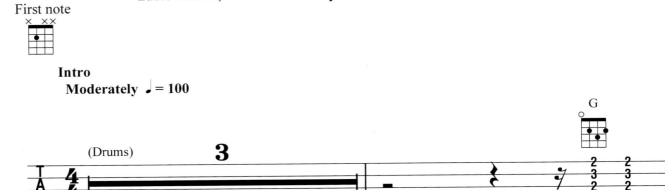

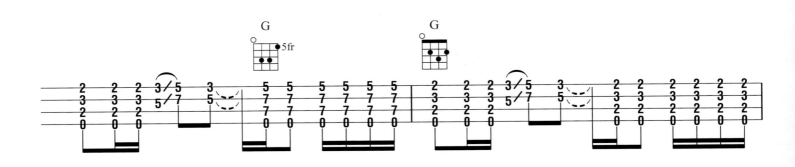

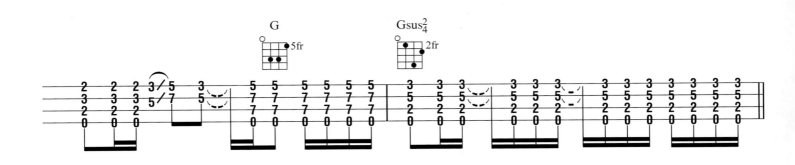

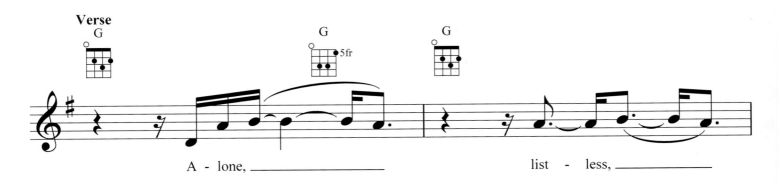

break - fast ta - ble in an oth - er - wise emp - ty room. ___

___ Young ___ girl, _____ vi - o - lins, _____

cen - ter of her own at - ten - tion. _____

Moth - er reads a - loud, ___ child tries _____ to un - der - stand _ it, ___

___ tries to make ___ her _____ proud. _____

Pre-Chorus

The shades ___ go _____ down. It's in _____ her ___ head, ___

5

Chorus

_____ paint - ed _____ room, _____ can't _____ de - ny _____ there's some - thing wrong. _____ Don't call _____ me daugh - ter, _____ not fit _____ to. The pic - ture kept will re - mind _____ me. Don't call _____ me daugh - ter, _____ not fit _____ to. The pic - ture kept will re - mind _____ me. Don't call _____ me...

Interlude

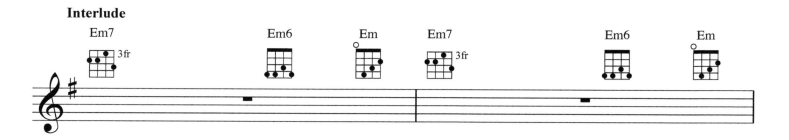

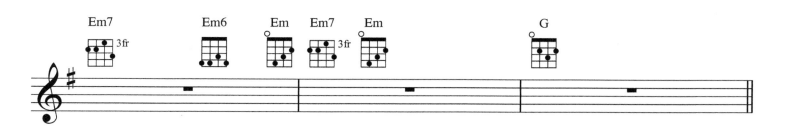

Bridge

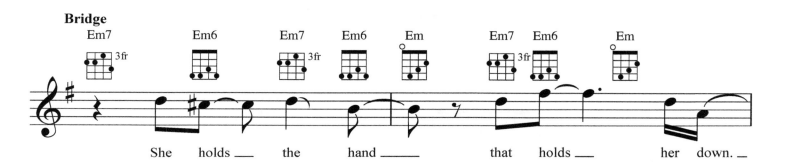

She holds ___ the hand ___ that holds ___ her down. ___

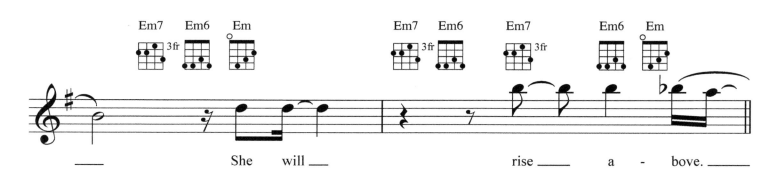

___ She will ___ rise ___ a - bove. ___

Guitar Solo

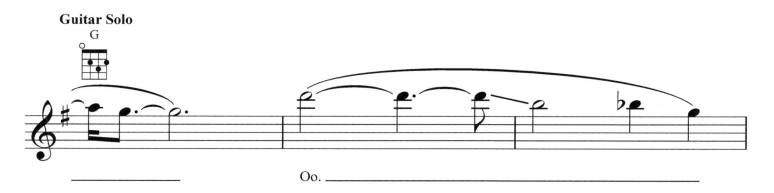

___ Oo. ___

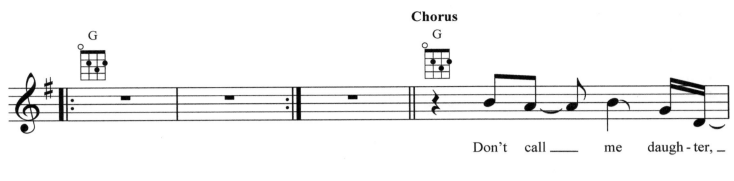

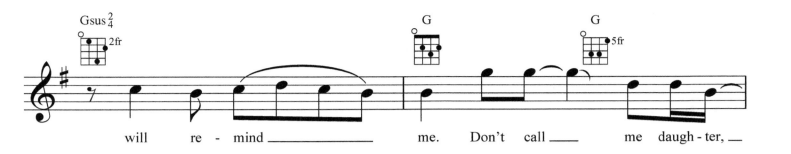

will re - mind _____ me. Don't call ____ me daugh - ter, __

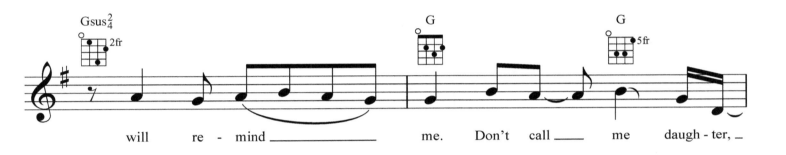

____ not fit _____ to. The pic - ture kept

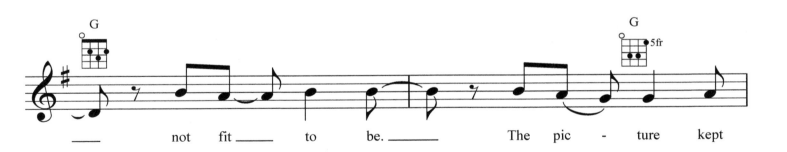

will re - mind _____ me. Don't call ____ me daugh - ter, __

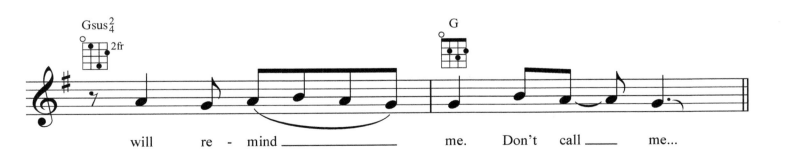

____ not fit _____ to be. _____ The pic - ture kept

will re - mind _____ me. Don't call ____ me...

Interlude

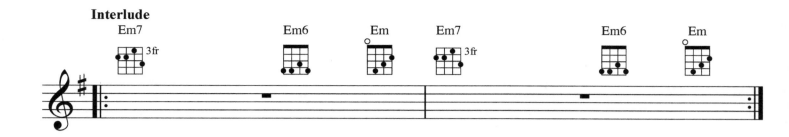

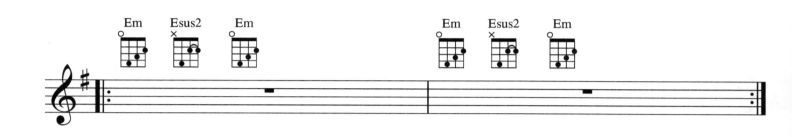

Outro

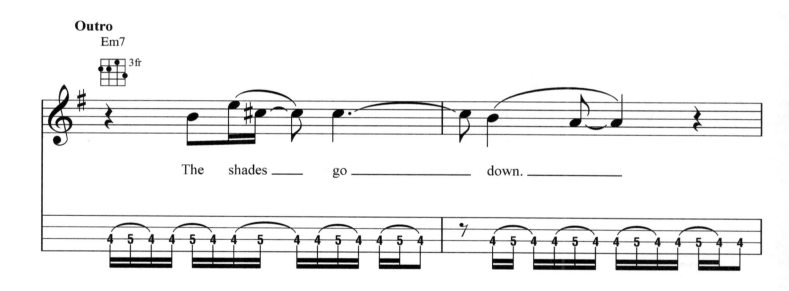

The shades _____ go _____ down. _____

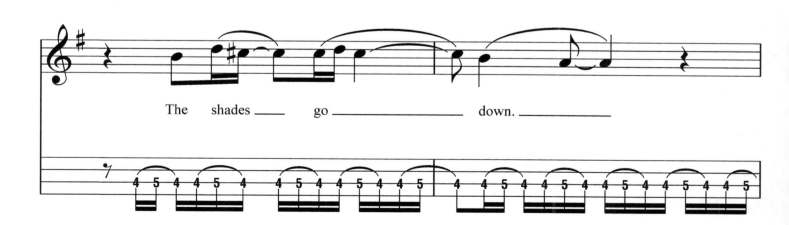

The shades _____ go _____ down. _____

The   shades   ____   go,   go, ____

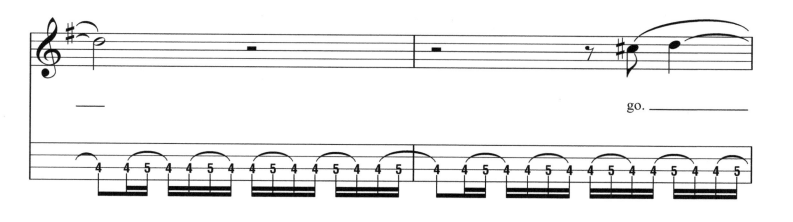

go. ____

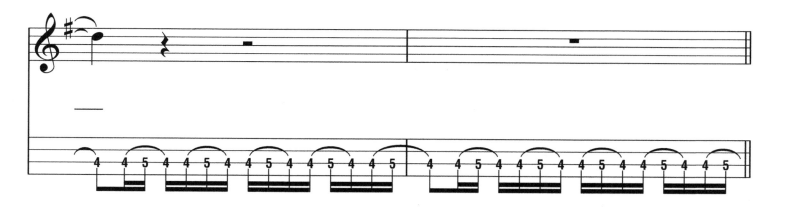

Play 4 times and fade

Hallelujah

Words and Music by Leonard Cohen

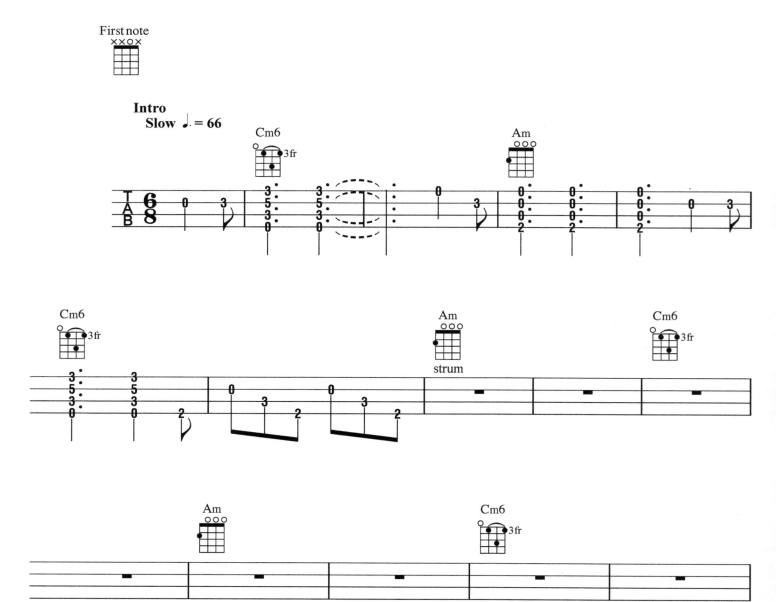

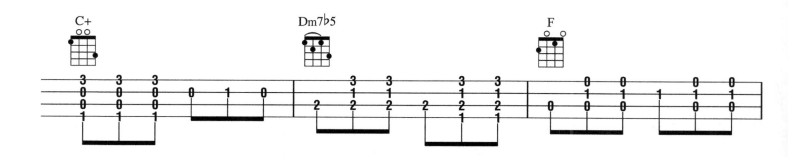

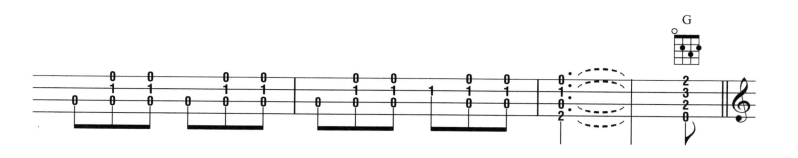

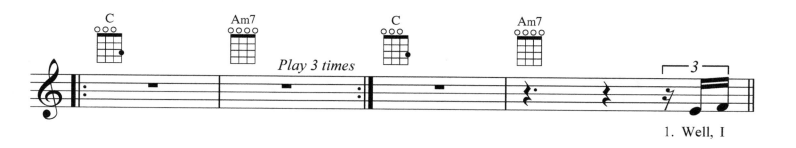

Play 3 times

1. Well, I

Verse

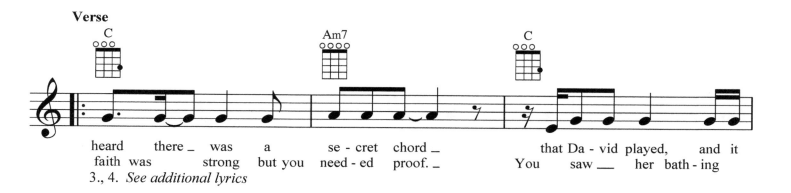

heard there _ was a se - cret chord _ that Da - vid played, and it
faith was strong but you need - ed proof. _ You saw _ her bath - ing

3., 4. *See additional lyrics*

pleased the Lord, ____ but you don't _ real - ly care for mu - sic
on the roof. Her beau - ty ____ and the moon - light o - ver -

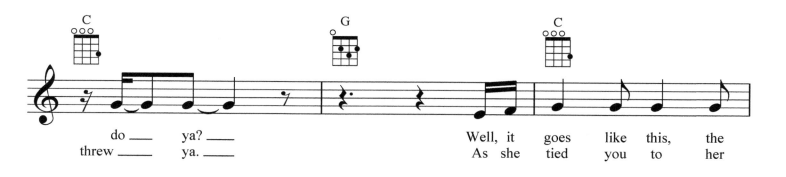

do ___ ya? ___ Well, it goes like this, the
threw ____ ya. ___ As she tied you to her

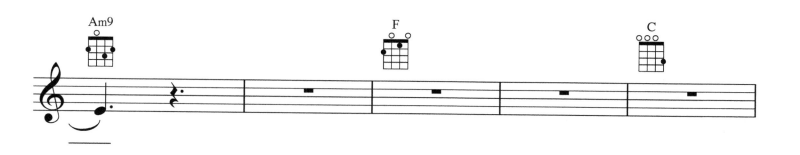

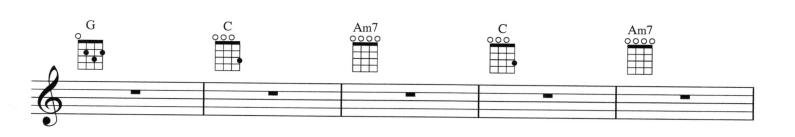

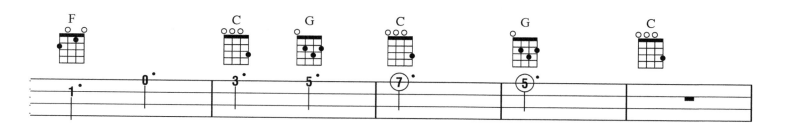

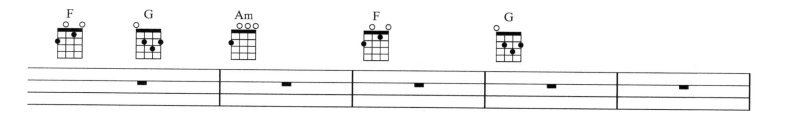

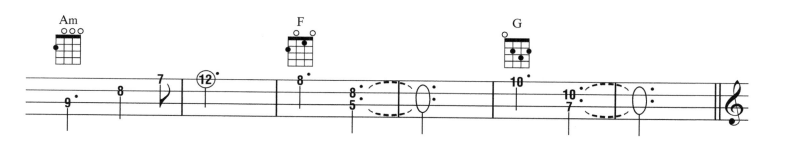

Verse

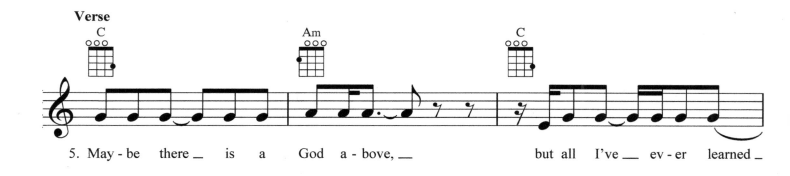

5. May - be there __ is a God a - bove, __ but all I've __ ev - er learned __

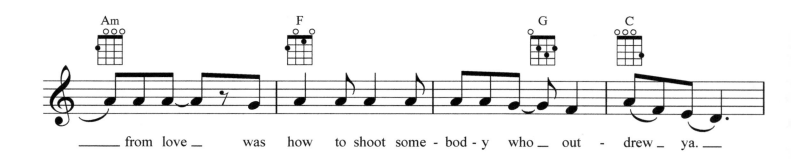

___ from love __ was how to shoot some - bod - y who __ out - drew __ ya. __

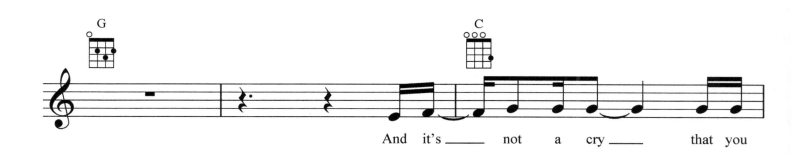

And it's _____ not a cry _____ that you

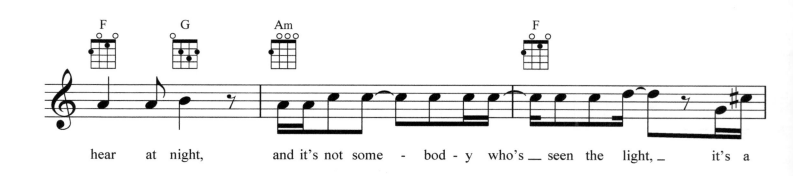

hear at night, and it's not some - bod - y who's __ seen the light, __ it's a

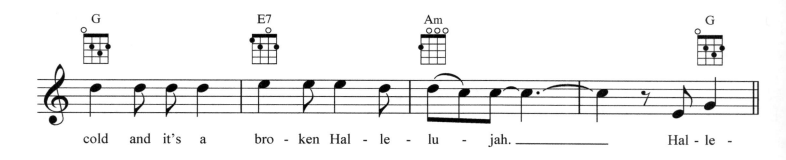

cold and it's a bro - ken Hal - le - lu - jah. _____ Hal - le -

Chorus

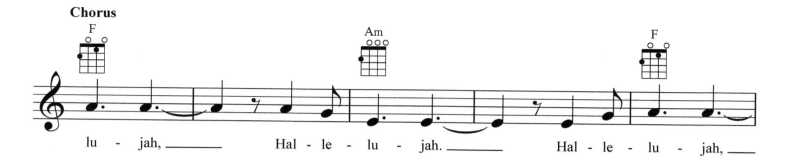

lu - jah, _____ Hal - le - lu - jah. _____ Hal - le - lu - jah, _____

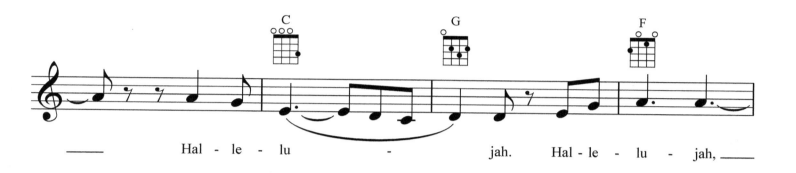

_____ Hal - le - lu - jah. Hal - le - lu - jah, _____

_____ Hal - le - lu - jah. _____ Hal - le - lu - jah, _____

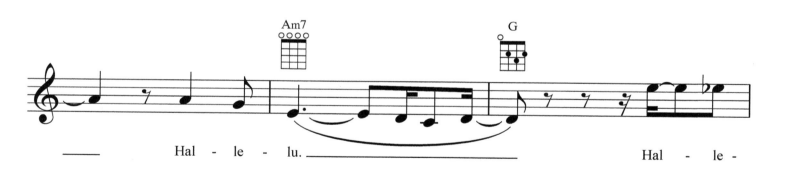

_____ Hal - le - lu. _____ Hal - le -

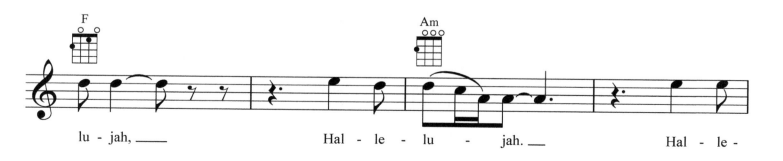

lu - jah, _____ Hal - le - lu - jah. _____ Hal - le -

lu - jah, _____ Hal - le - lu -

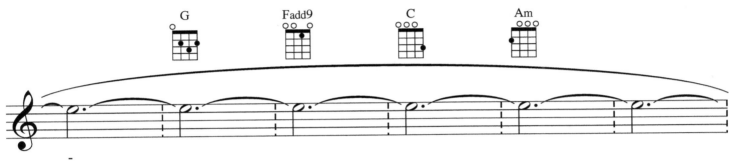

- jah. _____ Hal - le -

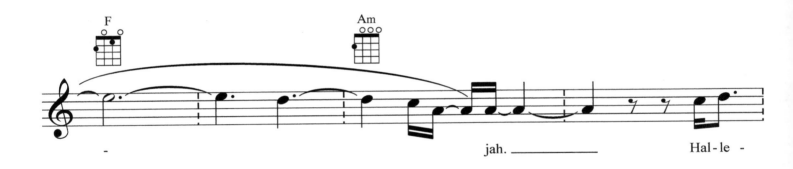

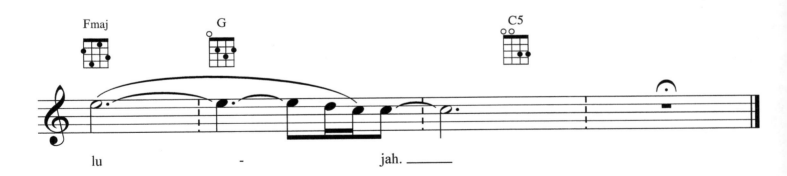

lu - jah. _____

Additional Lyrics

3. My baby, I've been here before.
   I've seen this room and I've walked this floor.
   You know, I used to live alone before I knew ya.
   And I've seen your flag on the marble arch,
   And love is not a vict'ry march,
   It's a cold and it's a broken Hallelujah.

4. Well, there was a time when you let me know
   What's really going on below,
   But now you never show that to me, do ya?
   But remember when I moved in you,
   And the Holy Dove was moving too,
   And ev'ry breath we drew was Hallelujah.

Iris

from the Motion Picture CITY OF ANGELS
Words and Music by John Rzeznik

First note

Intro

Moderately slow ♩ = 51

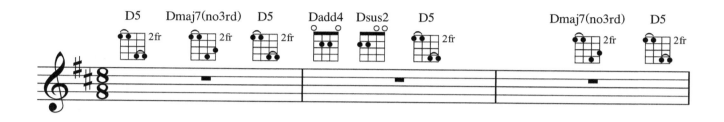

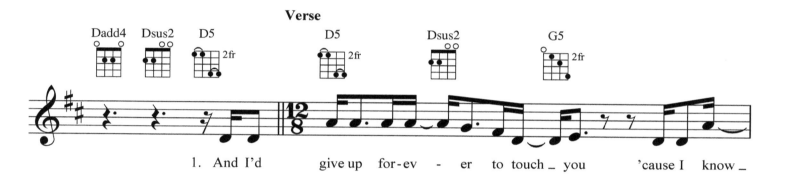

1. And I'd   give up for-ev - er to touch _ you   'cause I know _

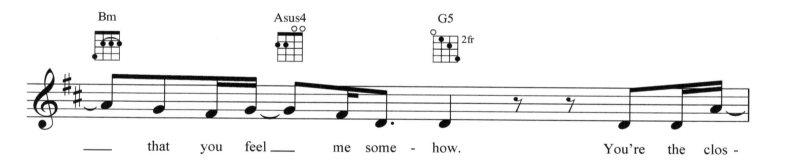

____ that you feel ___ me some - how.   You're the clos -

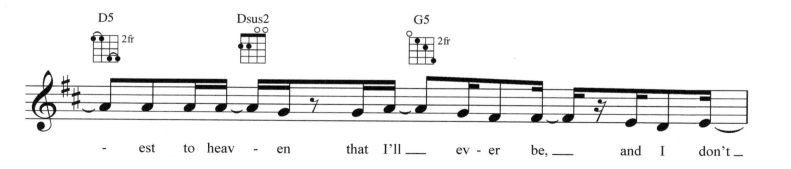

- est to heav - en that I'll ___ ev - er be, ___ and I don't _

_____ wan-na go _____ home right now.   And all _____ I can taste _____ is this mo-ment,   and all _____

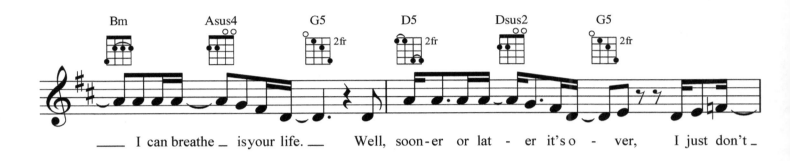

_____ I can breathe _____ is your life. _____   Well, soon-er or lat - er it's o - ver,   I just don't _____

𝄋 Chorus

_____ wan-na miss _____ you to-night. _____   And I   don't want the world _____ to see _____ me 'cause I don't _____

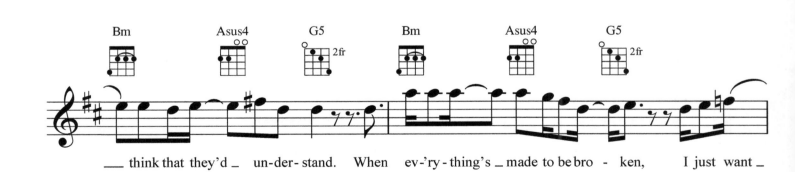

_____ think that they'd _____ un-der-stand.   When ev-'ry-thing's _____ made to be bro - ken,   I just want _____

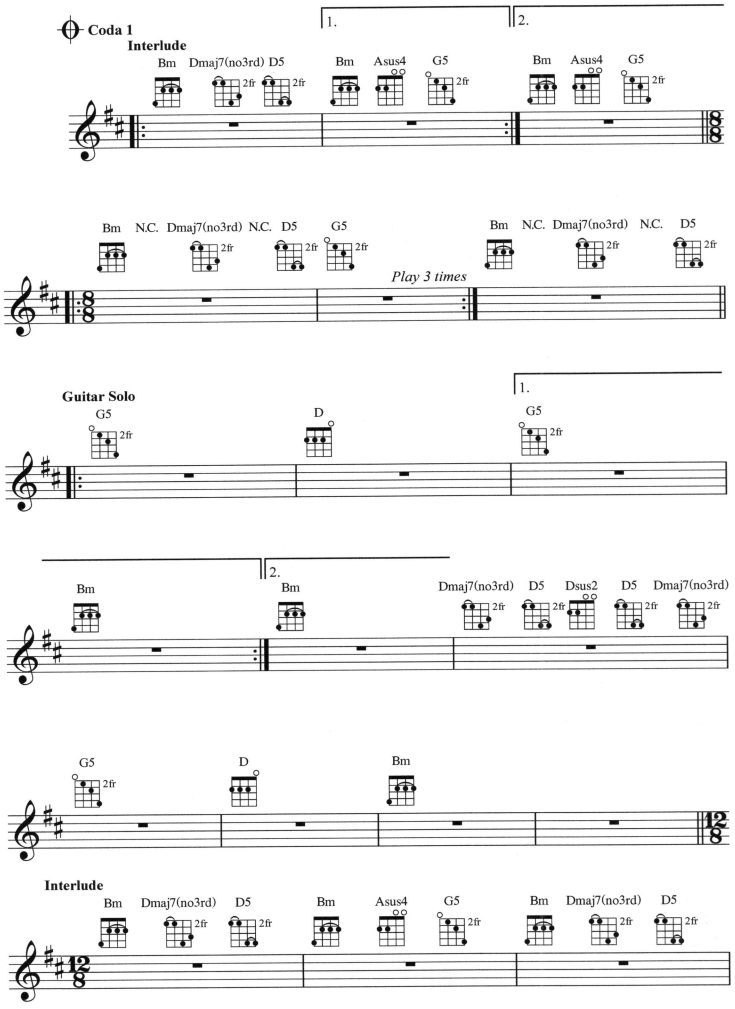

Ho Hey

Words and Music by Jeremy Fraites and Wesley Schultz

I been sleep - in' in _____ my bed, _____
I don't know where I _____ went wrong, _____
I'd be stand - in' on _____ Ca - nal _____

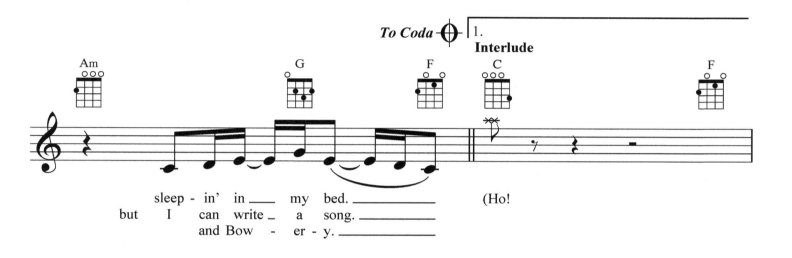

To Coda ⊕ | 1.

Interlude

sleep - in' in ___ my bed. _____ (Ho!
but I can write _ a song. _____
and Bow - er - y. _____

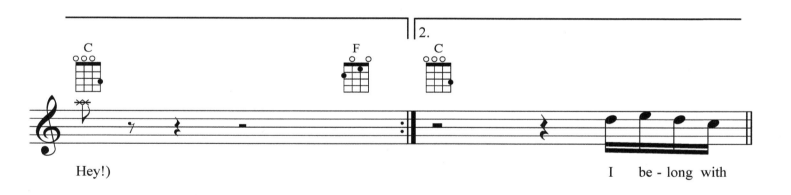

| 2.

Hey!) I be - long with

Chorus

Double-time feel

you, you be - long with me. You're my ___ sweet - heart. _ I be - long with

you,   you be-long with me. You're my ___ sweet...

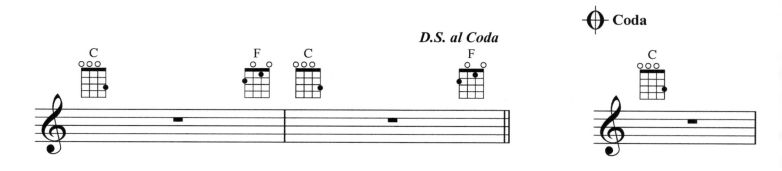

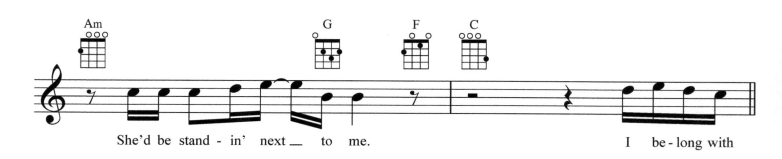

She'd be stand-in' next ___ to me.   I be-long with

Chorus
Double-time feel

you,   you be-long with me. You're my ___ sweet - heart. ___   I be-long with

you,   you be-long with me. You're my ___ sweet - heart. ___   Love, ___

Bridge

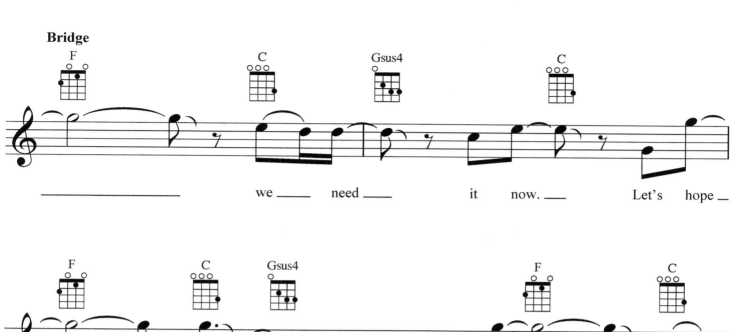

_____ we ___ need ___ it now. ___ Let's hope ___

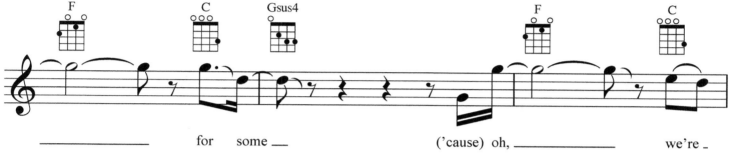

_____ for some ___ ('cause) oh, _____ we're _

Chorus

bleed - in' out. ___ I be - long with you, you be - long with me. You're my ___ sweet -

End double-time feel

- heart. ___ I be - long with you, you be - long with me. You're my ___ sweet...

Outro

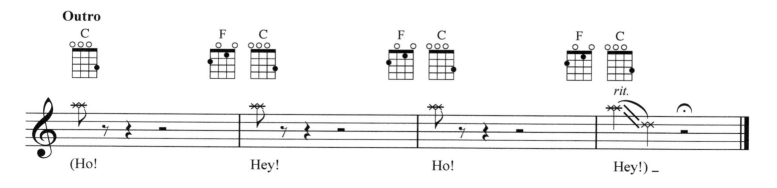

(Ho! Hey! Ho! Hey!) _

The Lazy Song

Words and Music by Bruno Mars, Ari Levine,
Philip Lawrence and Keinan Warsame

First note

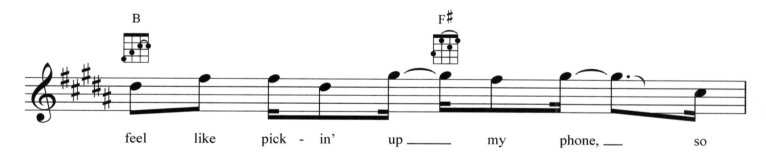

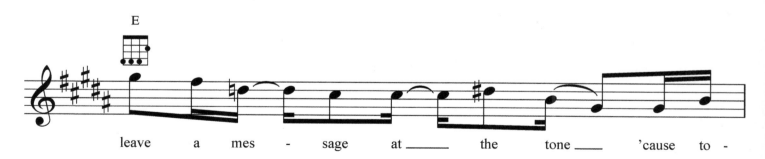

day I swear I'm not do-in' an - y-thing. Ah. 1. I'm gon-na

Verse

kick my feet up then stare at the fan, _____ meet a
I'll wake up, do some P - Nine - ty - X,

turn the T - V on, throw my hand in my pants. _____ And
real - ly nice girl, have some real - ly nice sex.

No - bod - y's go'n' tell me I can't, _____ no. I'll be
she's gon - na scream out, "This is great!" ___ Yeah, I

loung - in' on the couch just chill - in' in my Snug - gie,
might mess a - round get my col - lege de - gree. I

click to M - T - V so they can teach me how to doug - ie. 'Cause
bet my old man will be so proud of me. But

29

in my cas - tle, I'm the frick - in' _____ man. _____ }
sor - ry, Pops, you'll just have to wait. _____ } Oh, ___

Pre-Chorus

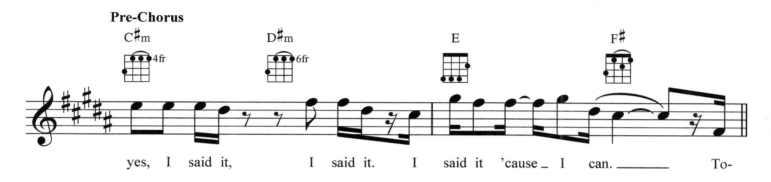

yes, I said it, I said it. I said it 'cause _ I can. _____ To-

% **Chorus**

day I don't feel like do - in' an - y - thing.

I just wan - na lay in my bed. _____ Don't

feel like pick - in' up _____ my phone, ___ so

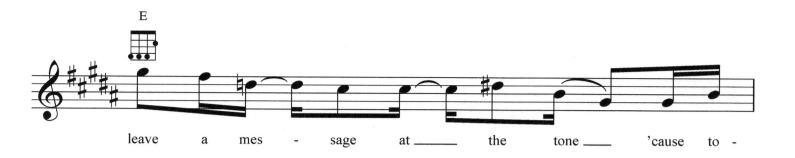

leave a mes - sage at _____ the tone _____ 'cause to -

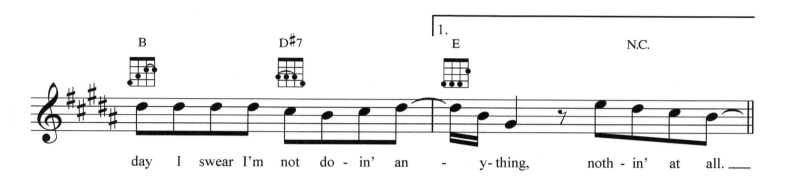

1.

day I swear I'm not do - in' an - y- thing, noth - in' at all. _____

Interlude

_____ Woo, hoo, _____ woo, hoo, _____ hoo. _____ Noth - in' at all. _____

To Coda ⊕

_____ Woo, hoo, _____ woo, hoo, _____ hoo. _____ 2. To-mor-row

2.

Bridge

- y- thing. No, I ain't gon - na comb my hair 'cause

I ain't go-in' an-y-where,   no, no, no, no, no, no, no, ___ no, no,

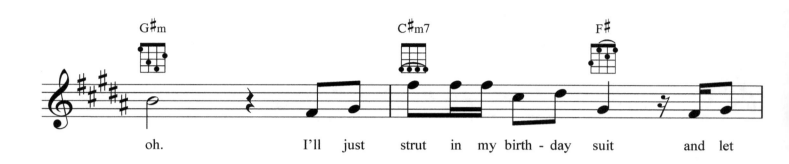

oh.   I'll just strut in my birth-day suit   and let

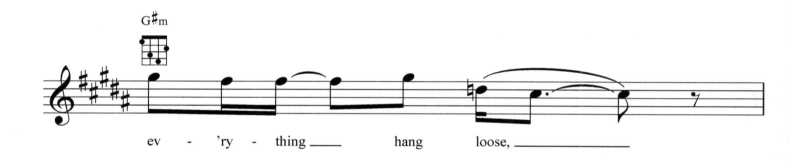

ev - 'ry - thing ___ hang loose, _____

D.S. al Coda
(take 1st ending)

yeah, yeah, yeah, yeah, yeah, yeah, yeah, _ yeah, yeah,   yeah. _   Oh, _____ to-

$\oplus$ **Coda**

hoo. _____ Noth - in' at all. _____

Wonderwall

Words and Music by Noel Gallagher

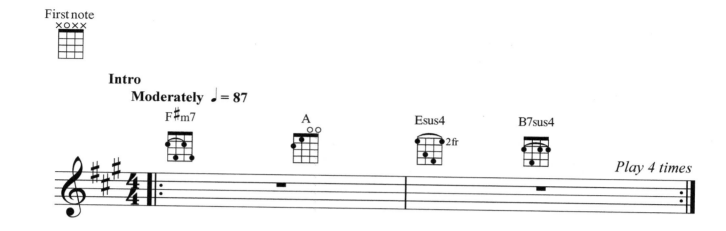

1. To - day is gon - na be the day that they're

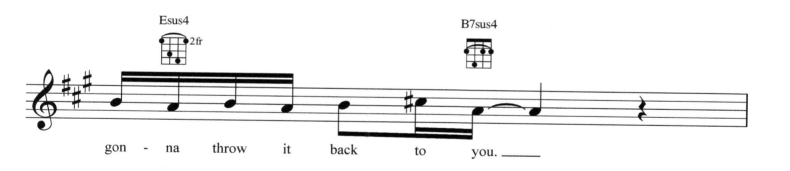

gon - na throw it back to you. _____

By now you should have some - how re - al -

ized   what   you   got - ta do. _____

I   don't   be - lieve ____   that an - y - bod - y

feels _   the way   I   do ____   a - bout you now. _____

Verse

2. Back - beat,   the word   is   on   the street   that the
3. To - day   was gon - na be   the day,   but they'll

fire _____   in   your   heart   is   out. _____
nev - er   throw   it   back   to   you. _____

I'm   sure   you've heard   it   all   be - fore,   but you
By   now   you   should have some - how   re - al -

Rolling in the Deep

Words and Music by Adele Adkins and Paul Epworth

your ____ love re - mind me of ____ us. They keep me

think - ing that we al - most had it all. The scars of

your ____ love, they leave me breath - less. I can't help

% Chorus

feel - ing we could have had it all. ____

Voc. Fig. 1

(You're gon - na wish you

Roll - ing in the deep. ____

nev - er had met me. Tears are gon - na fall

Verse

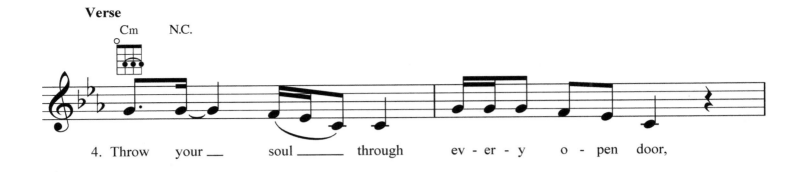

4. Throw your ___ soul ___ through ev - er - y o - pen door,

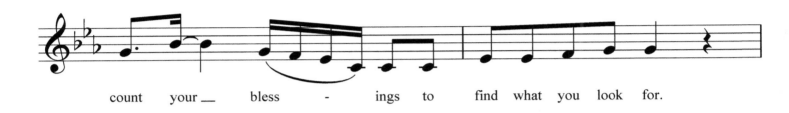

count your ___ bless - ings to find what you look for.

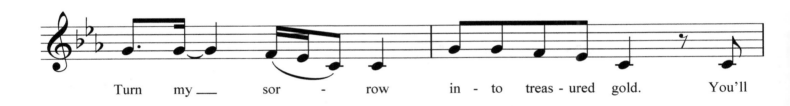

Turn my ___ sor - row in - to treas - ured gold. You'll

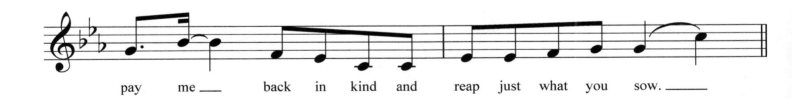

pay me ___ back in kind and reap just what you sow. ___

Chorus

Bkgd. Voc.: w/ Voc. Fig. 1 (2 times)

We could have had it all. ___

We could have had it all, _____

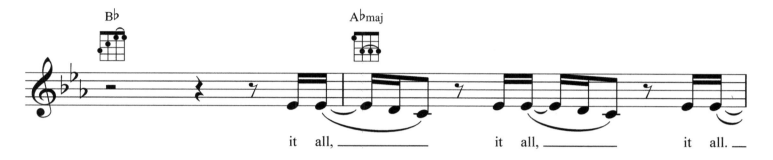

it all, _____ it all, _____ it all. __

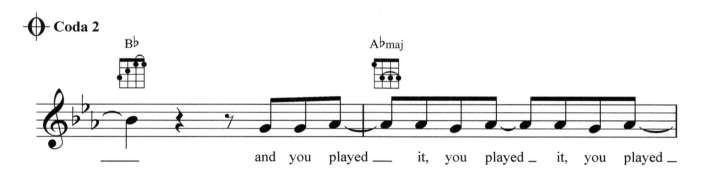

⊕ **Coda 1**

D.S. al Coda 1

D.S. al Coda 2

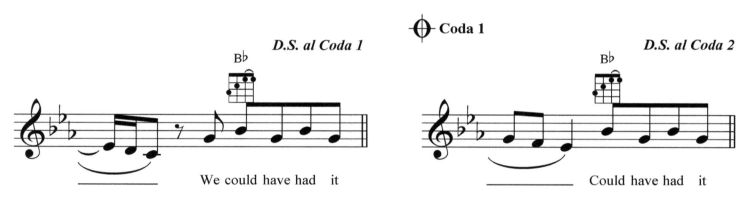

We could have had it

_____ Could have had it

⊕ **Coda 2**

_____ and you played __ it, you played __ it, you played __

_____ it, you played __ it to the beat. _____

The Scientist

**Words and Music by Guy Berryman, Jon Buckland,
Will Champion and Chris Martin**

you,   tell   you   I'll   set _____ you   a - part. _____

- ress   that   most speak as   loud _____ as   my   heart. _____

_____ Tell   me   your   se -   crets   and ask   me   your   ques -

_____ Tell   me   you   love _____ me, _____ come back   and   haunt __

- tions,   oh,   let's   go   back   to   the   start. _____

_____ me,   oh,   and   I   rush   to   the   start. _____

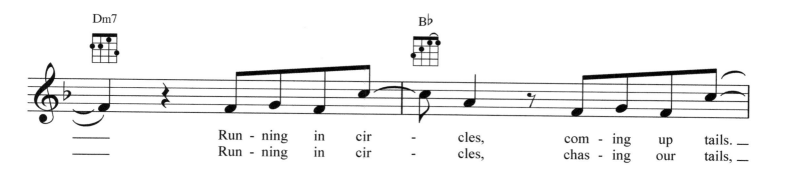

_____ Run - ning   in   cir   -   cles,   com - ing   up   tails. __

_____ Run - ning   in   cir   -   cles,   chas - ing   our   tails, __

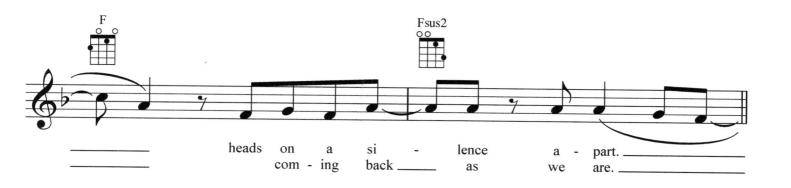

_____ heads   on   a   si -   lence   a - part. _____

_____ com - ing   back _____ as   we   are. _____

Chorus

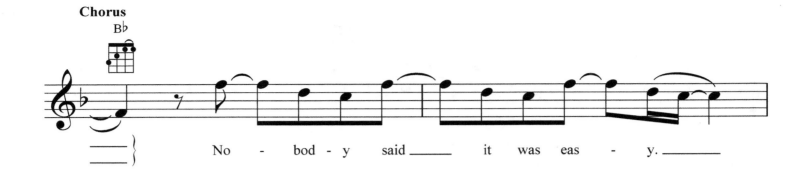

No - bod - y said ____ it was eas - y. ____

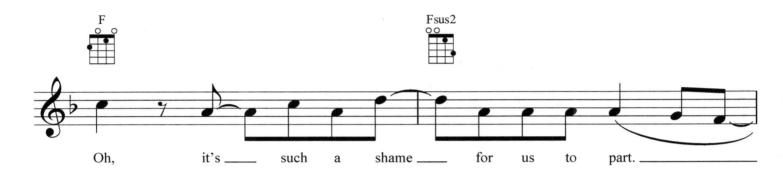

Oh, it's ____ such a shame ____ for us to part. ____

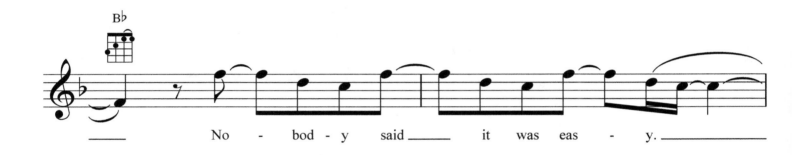

____ No - bod - y said ____ it was eas - y. ____

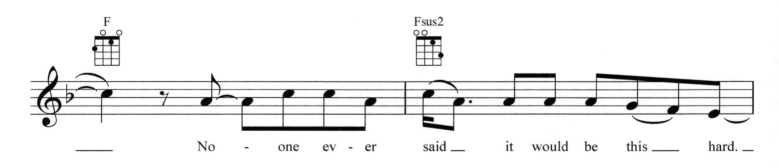

____ No - one ev - er said __ it would be this ____ hard. ____

Oh, take me back to the start. _____

Some Nights

Words and Music by Jeff Bhasker, Andrew Dost,
Jack Antonoff and Nate Ruess

still   wake __ up, _____   I   still   see   your __   ghost. __   Oh   Lord,   I'm

still   not __ sure _____   what   I   stand   for, ___   oh. ____

Voc. Fig. 1

Whoa, __

What   do   I   stand   for? _   What   do   I   stand   for? _   Most   nights, _   I   don't

End Voc. Fig. 1

oh. _____   Whoa, _   oh. _____

Interlude

Voc. Fig. 2

know ___   an - y   more. _____

know ___   an - y   more. _____
(Oh. _____   Whoa, _   oh. _____   Whoa, _

Verse

right; (That's all right.) I found a mar-tyr in ___ my bed ___ to-night. ___ She

stops my bones from won-der-in' just who I am, ___ who I ___ am, who I

am. _____ Oh, who am I? _____ Mm, _____

___ mm. _____ Well,

Chorus

some nights ___ I wish ___ that this all ___ would end _____ 'cause

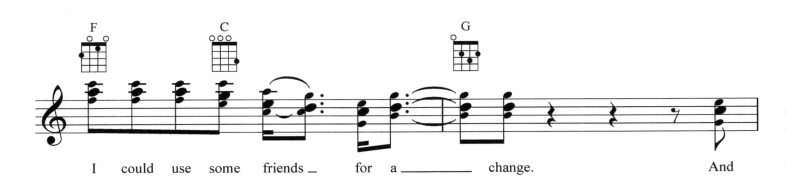

I could use some friends _ for a _____ change.   And

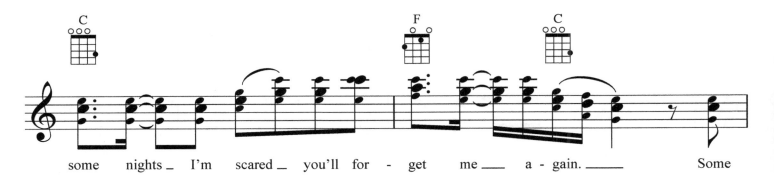

some nights _ I'm scared _ you'll for - get me __ a - gain. _____   Some

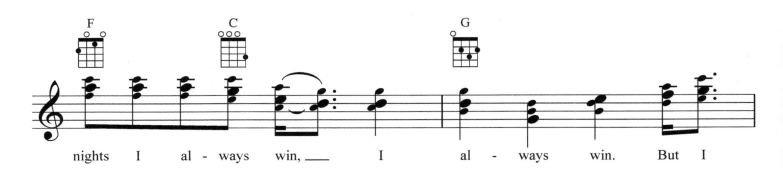

nights I al - ways win, ____   I   al - ways   win.   But I

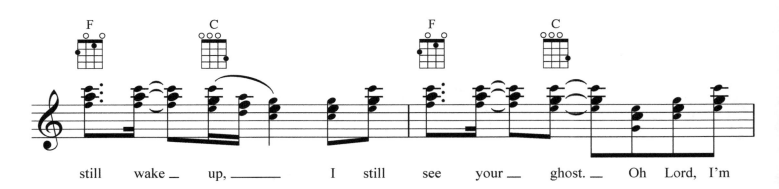

still wake _ up, _____   I still   see   your _ ghost. _ Oh Lord, I'm

Bkgd. Voc. w/ Voc. Fig. 1

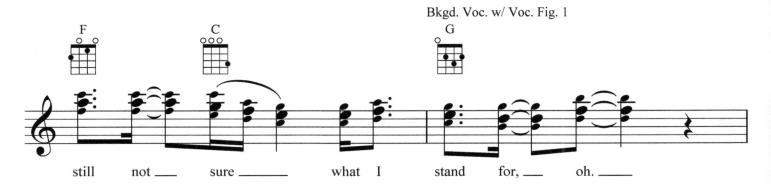

still not ___ sure _____   what I   stand for, __ oh. ____

52

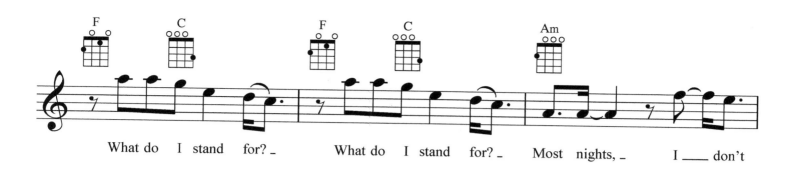

What do I stand for? _ What do I stand for? _ Most nights, _ I ___ don't

Bridge

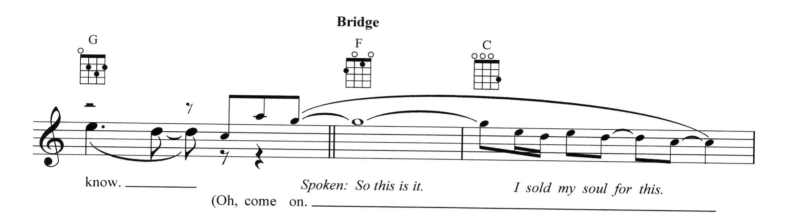

know. _____ *Spoken: So this is it.* *I sold my soul for this.*
(Oh, come on. _____

Washed my hands of that for this. I miss my mom and dad for this? No, when I see stars, when
Ooh, _ na, ___ na. Ah, ooh, _ na, ___ na, come on. _____

I see, when I see stars, that's all they are. When I hear songs... they

___ Ah, ooh, na, ___ na. Ooh, na, ___ na.

sound   like ___   this   one, so   come   on. _____

Ooh,   na, ___   na.   Oh,   come   on.) ___

D.S. al Coda

Oh, ___ come   on.   3. Well,

(Oh,   come   on.) _____

Coda

dried   up   in   the   des - ert   sun? ____   My   heart   is

Bridge

break - ing   for ____   my   sis - ter _____   and   the

con   that   she ____   called   "love." ____   And   then   I

54

look in - to _____ my neph - ew's eyes, _____

man, you would - n't be - lieve _____

the most a - maz - ing things

that can come from _____

_____ some ter - ri - ble _____

Interlude

lies. _____

Ahh. _____   Ahh. _____

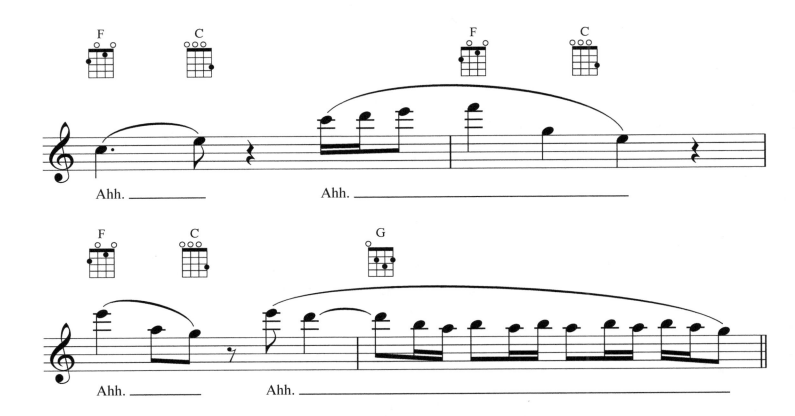

Ahh. _____   Ahh. _____

Ahh. _____   Ahh. _____

Interlude
Bkgd. Voc. w/ Voc. Fig. 2 (2times)

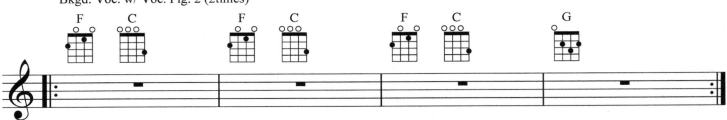

Outro-Verse

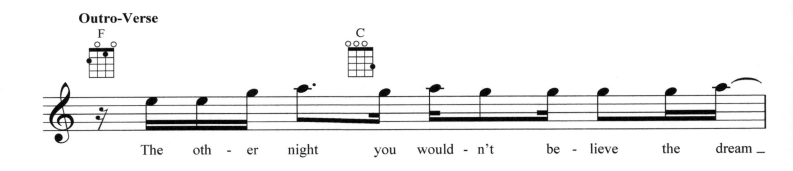

The oth - er night you would - n't be - lieve the dream _

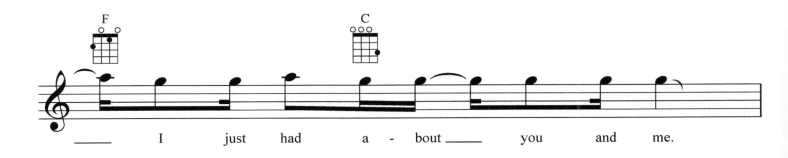

_____ I just had a - bout _____ you and me.

I called you up but we both a - gree.

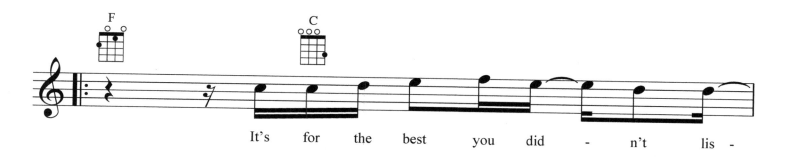

It's for the best you did - n't lis -

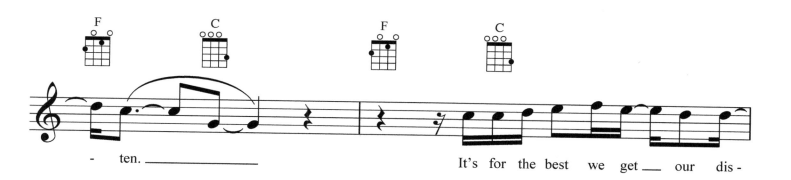

- ten. _____ It's for the best we get __ our dis-

Bkgd. Voc. w/ Voc. Fig. 2 (2times)

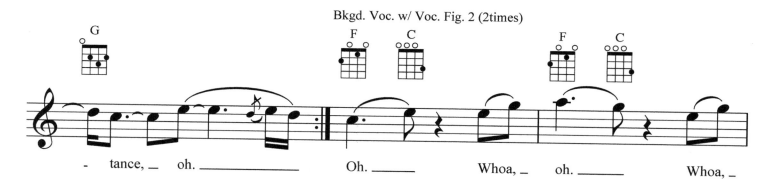

- tance, _ oh. _____ Oh. _____ Whoa, _ oh. _____ Whoa, _

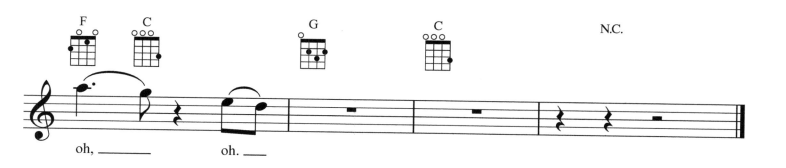

oh, _____ oh. ___

You and I

Words and Music by Ingrid Michaelson

First note

Intro
Moderately fast ♩ = 138

Verse

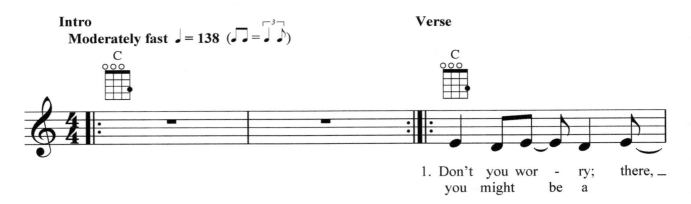

1. Don't you wor - ry; there, ___
   you might be a

___ my hon - ey. We might not ___ have an - y mon - ey
bit con-fused and you ___ might be a lit - tle bit bruised but

but we've got ___ our love ___ to pay the bills. ___
ba - by, how ___ we spoon ___ like no one else. ___

So May - be I think you're cute and fun - ny; may -
    I will help you read those books if

- be I wan - na do what bun - nies do with you, if you
you will soothe my wor - ried looks, and we will put the lone -

know what I mean.
- some on the shelf.

Oh,

*§ **Chorus**

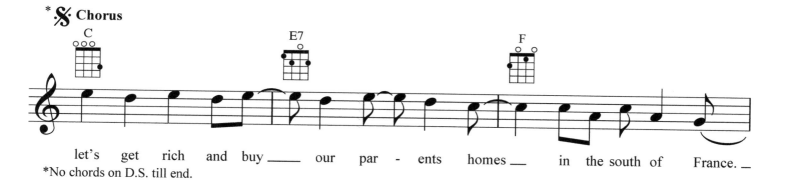

let's get rich and buy our par - ents homes in the south of France.
*No chords on D.S. till end.

Let's get rich and give ev - 'ry - bod - y nice sweat - ers and teach

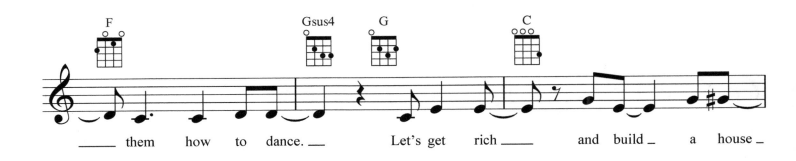

_____ them how to dance. _____ Let's get rich _____ and build_ a house _____

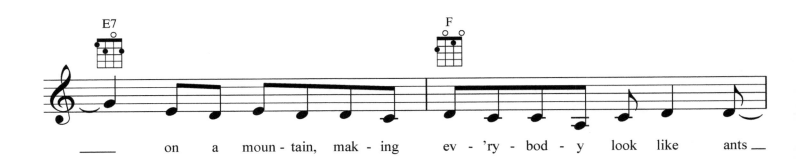

_____ on a moun-tain, mak-ing ev-'ry-bod-y look like ants _____

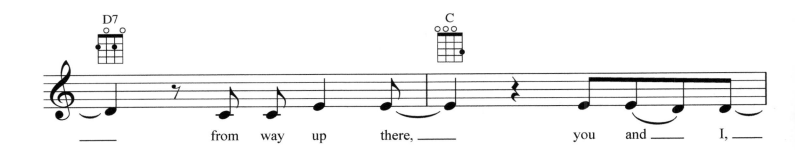

_____ from way up there, _____ you and _____ I, _____

To Coda ⊕ |1.

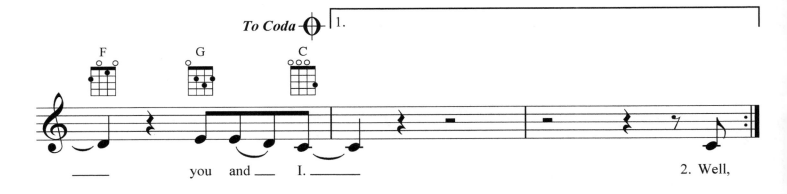

_____ you and _ I. _____ 2. Well,

|2.   *D.S. al Coda*   ⊕ **Coda**

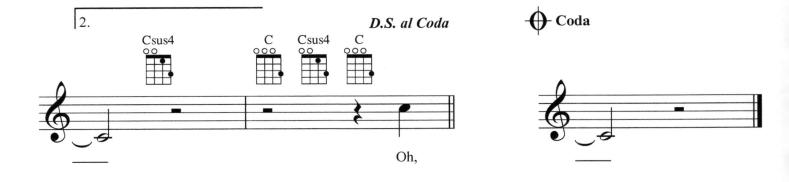

Oh,   _____

The Best Collections for Ukulele

The Best Songs Ever

70 songs have now been arranged for ukulele. Includes: Always • Bohemian Rhapsody • Memory • My Favorite Things • Over the Rainbow • Piano Man • What a Wonderful World • Yesterday • You Raise Me Up • and more.

00282413 . . . . $17.99

Campfire Songs for Ukulele

30 favorites to sing as you roast marshmallows and strum your uke around the campfire. Includes: God Bless the U.S.A. • Hallelujah • The House of the Rising Sun • I Walk the Line • Puff the Magic Dragon • Wagon Wheel • You Are My Sunshine • and more.

00129170 . . . . $14.99

The Daily Ukulele

arr. Liz and Jim Beloff
Strum a different song everyday with easy arrangements of 365 of your favorite songs in one big songbook! Includes favorites by the Beatles, Beach Boys, and Bob Dylan, folk songs, pop songs, kids' songs, Christmas carols, and Broadway and Hollywood tunes, all with a spiral binding for ease of use.

00240356 Original Edition $39.99
00240681 Leap Year Edition $39.99
00119270 Portable Edition $37.50

Disney Hits for Ukulele

Play 23 of your favorite Disney songs on your ukulele. Includes: The Bare Necessities • Cruella De Vil • Do You Want to Build a Snowman? • Kiss the Girl • Lava • Let It Go • Once upon a Dream • A Whole New World • and more.

00151250 . . . . $16.99

Also available:

00291547 **Disney Fun Songs for Ukulele** . . . $16.99
00701708 **Disney Songs for Ukulele** $14.99
00334696 **First 50 Disney Songs on Ukulele** . $16.99

First 50 Songs You Should Play on Ukulele

An amazing collec-tion of 50 accessible, must-know favorites: Edelweiss • Hey, Soul Sister • I Walk the Line • I'm Yours • Imagine • Over the Rainbow • Peaceful Easy Feeling • The Rainbow Connection • Riptide • more.

00149250 . . . . $16.99

Also available:

00292082 **First 50 Melodies on Ukulele** . . . $15.99
00289029 **First 50 Songs on Solo Ukulele** . . $15.99
00347437 **First 50 Songs to Strum on Uke** . $16.99

40 Most Streamed Songs for Ukulele

40 top hits that sound great on uke! Includes: Despacito • Feel It Still • Girls like You • Happier • Havana • High Hopes • The Middle • Perfect • 7 Rings • Shallow • Shape of You • Something Just like This • Stay • Sucker • Sunflower • Sweet but Psycho • Thank U, Next • There's Nothing Holdin' Me Back • Without Me • and more!

00298113 . . . . $17.99

The 4 Chord Songbook

With just 4 chords, you can play 50 hot songs on your ukulele! Songs include: Brown Eyed Girl • Do Wah Diddy Diddy • Hey Ya! • Ho Hey • Jessie's Girl • Let It Be • One Love • Stand by Me • Toes • With or Without You • and many more.

00142050 . . . . $16.99

Also available:

00141143 **The 3-Chord Songbook** $16.99

Pop Songs for Kids

30 easy pop favorites for kids to play on uke, including: Brave • Can't Stop the Feeling! • Feel It Still • Fight Song • Happy • Havana • House of Gold • How Far I'll Go • Let It Go • Remember Me (Ernesto de la Cruz) • Rewrite the Stars • Roar • Shake It Off • Story of My Life • What Makes You Beautiful • and more.

00284415 . . . . $16.99

Simple Songs for Ukulele

50 favorites for standard G-C-E-A ukulele tuning, including: All Along the Watchtower • Can't Help Falling in Love • Don't Worry, Be Happy • Ho Hey • I'm Yours • King of the Road • Sweet Home Alabama • You Are My Sunshine • and more.

00156815 . . . . $14.99

Also available:

00276644 **More Simple Songs for Ukulele** . $14.99

Top Hits of 2020

18 uke-friendly tunes of 2020 are featured in this collection of melody, lyric and chord arrangements in standard G-C-E-A tuning. Includes: Adore You (Harry Styles) • Before You Go (Lewis Capaldi) • Cardigan (Taylor Swift) • Daisies (Katy Perry) • I Dare You (Kelly Clarkson) • Level of Concern (twenty one pilots) • No Time to Die (Billie Eilish) • Rain on Me (Lady Gaga feat. Ariana Grande) • Say So (Doja Cat) • and more.

00355553 . . . . $14.99

Also available:

00302274 **Top Hits of 2019** $14.99

Ukulele: The Most Requested Songs

Strum & Sing Series
Cherry Lane Music
Nearly 50 favorites all expertly arranged for ukulele! Includes: Bubbly • Build Me Up, Buttercup • Cecilia • Georgia on My Mind • Kokomo • L-O-V-E • Your Body Is a Wonderland • and more.

02501453 . . . . $14.99

The Ultimate Ukulele Fake Book

Uke enthusiasts will love this giant, spiral-bound collection of over 400 songs for uke! Includes: Crazy • Dancing Queen • Downtown • Fields of Gold • Happy • Hey Jude • 7 Years • Summertime • Thinking Out Loud • Thriller • Wagon Wheel • and more.

00175500 9" x 12" Edition $45.00
00319997 5.5" x 8.5" Edition $39.99

HAL•LEONARD
UKULELE PLAY-ALONG

Now you can play your favorite songs on your uke with great-sounding backing tracks to help you sound like a bona fide pro! The audio also features playback tools so you can adjust the tempo without changing the pitch and loop challenging parts.

1. POP HITS
00701451 Book/CD Pack $15.99

3. HAWAIIAN FAVORITES
00701453 Book/Online Audio $14.99

4. CHILDREN'S SONGS
00701454 Book/Online Audio $14.99

5. CHRISTMAS SONGS
00701696 Book/CD Pack $12.99

6. LENNON & MCCARTNEY
00701723 Book/Online Audio $12.99

7. DISNEY FAVORITES
00701724 Book/Online Audio $14.99

8. CHART HITS
00701745 Book/CD Pack $15.99

9. THE SOUND OF MUSIC
00701784 Book/CD Pack $14.99

10. MOTOWN
00701964 Book/CD Pack $12.99

11. CHRISTMAS STRUMMING
00702458 Book/Online Audio $12.99

12. BLUEGRASS FAVORITES
00702584 Book/CD Pack $12.99

13. UKULELE SONGS
00702599 Book/CD Pack $12.99

14. JOHNNY CASH
00702615 Book/Online Audio $15.99

15. COUNTRY CLASSICS
00702834 Book/CD Pack $12.99

16. STANDARDS
00702835 Book/CD Pack $12.99

17. POP STANDARDS
00702836 Book/CD Pack $12.99

18. IRISH SONGS
00703086 Book/Online Audio $12.99

19. BLUES STANDARDS
00703087 Book/CD Pack $12.99

20. FOLK POP ROCK
00703088 Book/CD Pack $12.99

21. HAWAIIAN CLASSICS
00703097 Book/CD Pack $12.99

22. ISLAND SONGS
00703098 Book/CD Pack $12.99

23. TAYLOR SWIFT
00221966 Book/Online Audio $16.99

24. WINTER WONDERLAND
00101871 Book/CD Pack $12.99

25. GREEN DAY
00110398 Book/CD Pack $14.99

26. BOB MARLEY
00110399 Book/Online Audio $14.99

27. TIN PAN ALLEY
00116358 Book/CD Pack $12.99

28. STEVIE WONDER
00116736 Book/CD Pack $14.99

29. OVER THE RAINBOW & OTHER FAVORITES
00117076 Book/Online Audio $15.99

30. ACOUSTIC SONGS
00122336 Book/CD Pack $14.99

31. JASON MRAZ
00124166 Book/CD Pack $14.99

32. TOP DOWNLOADS
00127507 Book/CD Pack $14.99

33. CLASSICAL THEMES
00127892 Book/Online Audio $14.99

34. CHRISTMAS HITS
00128602 Book/CD Pack $14.99

35. SONGS FOR BEGINNERS
00129009 Book/Online Audio $14.99

36. ELVIS PRESLEY HAWAII
00138199 Book/Online Audio $14.99

37. LATIN
00141191 Book/Online Audio $14.99

38. JAZZ
00141192 Book/Online Audio $14.99

39. GYPSY JAZZ
00146559 Book/Online Audio $15.99

40. TODAY'S HITS
00160845 Book/Online Audio $14.99

HAL•LEONARD®
www.halleonard.com

Prices, contents, and availability subject to change without notice.

UKULELE ENSEMBLE SERIES

he songs in these collections are playable by any combination of ukuleles (soprano, concert, tenor or baritone). ach arrangement features the melody, a harmony part, and a "bass" line. Chord symbols are also provided if ou wish to add a rhythm part. For groups with more than three or four ukuleles, the parts may be doubled.

HE BEATLES
Mid-Intermediate Level
ll My Loving • Blackbird • Can't Buy Me Love • Eight Days a Week
Here, There and Everywhere • I Want to Hold Your Hand • Let It
e • Love Me Do • Norwegian Wood (This Bird Has Flown) • Penny
ane • Something • Ticket to Ride • When I'm Sixty-Four • Yellow
ubmarine • Yesterday.
0295927 .... $9.99

CHRISTMAS SONGS
arly Intermediate Level
he Chipmunk Song • The Christmas Song (Chestnuts Roasting on
n Open Fire) • Do You Hear What I Hear • Feliz Navidad • Frosty
he Snow Man • Have Yourself a Merry Little Christmas • Here
omes Santa Claus (Right Down Santa Claus Lane) • A Holly Jolly
hristmas • (There's No Place Like) Home for the Holidays • Jingle
ell Rock • The Little Drummer Boy • Merry Christmas, Darling • The
lost Wonderful Time of the Year • Silver Bells • White Christmas.
0129247 .... $9.99

CLASSIC ROCK
Mid-Intermediate Level
qualung • Behind Blue Eyes • Born to Be Wild • Crazy Train • Fly
ke an Eagle • Free Bird • Hey Jude • Low Rider • Moondance • Oye
omo Va • Proud Mary • (I Can't Get No) Satisfaction • Smoke on
he Water • Summertime Blues • Sunshine of Your Love.
0103904 .... $10.99

DISNEY FAVORITES
arly Intermediate Level
he Bare Necessities • Beauty and the Beast • Can You Feel the
ove Tonight • Colors of the Wind • A Dream Is a Wish Your Heart
lakes • It's a Small World • Let It Go • Let's Go Fly a Kite • Little
pril Shower • Mickey Mouse March • Seize the Day • The Siamese
at Song • Supercalifragilisticexpialidocious • Under the Sea • A
Vhole New World.
0279513 .... $9.99

HAWAIIAN SONGS
Mid-Intermediate Level
loha Oe • Beyond the Rainbow • Harbor Lights • Hawaiian War
hant (Ta-Hu-Wa-Hu-Wai) • The Hawaiian Wedding Song (Ke Kali
ei Au) • Ka-lu-a • Lovely Hula Hands • Mele Kalikimaka • The
loon of Manakoora • One Paddle, Two Paddle • Pearly Shells
upu 'O 'Ewa) • Red Sails in the Sunset • Sleepy Lagoon • Song of
he Islands • Tiny Bubbles.
0119254 .... $9.99

THE NUTCRACKER
Late Intermediate Level
Arabian Dance ("Coffee") • Chinese Dance ("Tea") • Dance of the
Reed-Flutes • Dance of the Sugar Plum Fairy • March • Overture •
Russian Dance ("Trepak") • Waltz of the Flowers.
00119908 .... $9.99

ROCK INSTRUMENTALS
Late Intermediate Level
Beck's Bolero • Cissy Strut • Europa (Earth's Cry Heaven's Smile) •
Frankenstein • Green Onions • Jessica • Misirlou • Perfidia • Pick Up
the Pieces • Pipeline • Rebel 'Rouser • Sleepwalk • Tequila • Walk
Don't Run • Wipe Out.
00103909 .... $9.99

STANDARDS & GEMS
Mid-Intermediate Level
Autumn Leaves • Cheek to Cheek • Easy to Love • Fly Me to the
Moon • I Only Have Eyes for You • It Had to Be You • Laura • Mack
the Knife • My Funny Valentine • Theme from "New York, New
York" • Over the Rainbow • Satin Doll • Some Day My Prince Will
Come • Summertime • The Way You Look Tonight.
00103898 .... $9.99

THEME MUSIC
Mid-Intermediate Level
Batman Theme • Theme from E.T. (The Extra-Terrestrial) • Forrest
Gump – Main Title (Feather Theme) • The Godfather (Love Theme)
• Hawaii Five-O Theme • He's a Pirate • Linus and Lucy • Mission:
Impossible Theme • Peter Gunn • The Pink Panther • Raiders March
• (Ghost) Riders in the Sky (A Cowboy Legend) • Theme from Spider
Man • Theme from "Star Trek®" • Theme from "Superman."
00103903 .... $10.99

www.halleonard.com

UKULELE CHORD SONGBOOKS

This series features convenient 6" x 9" books with complete lyrics and chord symbols for dozens of great songs. Each song also includes chord grids at the top of every page and the first notes of the melody for easy reference.

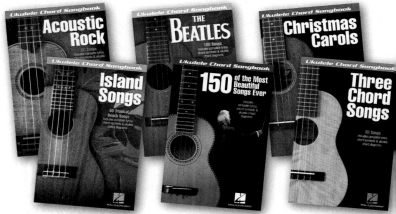

ACOUSTIC ROCK

60 tunes: American Pie • Band on the Run • Catch the Wind • Daydream • Every Rose Has Its Thorn • Hallelujah • Iris • More Than Words • Patience • The Sound of Silence • Space Oddity • Sweet Talkin' Woman • Wake up Little Susie • Who'll Stop the Rain • and more.
00702482 . . . . $15.99

THE BEATLES

100 favorites: Across the Universe • Carry That Weight • Dear Prudence • Good Day Sunshine • Here Comes the Sun • If I Fell • Love Me Do • Michelle • Ob-La-Di, Ob-La-Da • Revolution • Something • Ticket to Ride • We Can Work It Out • and many more.
00703065 . . . . $22.99

BEST SONGS EVER

70 songs: All I Ask of You • Bewitched • Edelweiss • Just the Way You Are • Let It Be • Memory • Moon River • Over the Rainbow • Someone to Watch over Me • Unchained Melody • You Are the Sunshine of My Life • You Raise Me Up • and more.
00117050 . . . . $16.99

CHILDREN'S SONGS

80 classics: Alphabet Song • "C" Is for Cookie • Do-Re-Mi • I'm Popeye the Sailor Man • Mickey Mouse March • Oh! Susanna • Polly Wolly Doodle • Puff the Magic Dragon • The Rainbow Connection • Sing • Three Little Fishies (Itty Bitty Poo) • and many more.
00702473 . . . . $17.99

CHRISTMAS CAROLS

75 favorites: Away in a Manger • Coventry Carol • The First Noel • Good King Wenceslas • Hark! the Herald Angels Sing • I Saw Three Ships • Joy to the World • O Little Town of Bethlehem • Still, Still, Still • Up on the Housetop • What Child Is This? • and more.
00702474 . . . . $14.99

CHRISTMAS SONGS

55 Christmas classics: Do They Know It's Christmas? • Frosty the Snow Man • Happy Xmas (War Is Over) • Jingle-Bell Rock • Little Saint Nick • The Most Wonderful Time of the Year • White Christmas • and more.
00101776 . . . . $14.99

ISLAND SONGS

60 beach party tunes: Blue Hawaii • Day-O (The Banana Boat Song) • Don't Worry, Be Happy • Island Girl • Kokomo • Lovely Hula Girl • Mele Kalikimaka • Red, Red Wine • Surfer Girl • Tiny Bubbles • Ukulele Lady • and many more.
00702471 . . . . $16.99

150 OF THE MOST BEAUTIFUL SONGS EVER

150 melodies: Always • Bewitched • Candle in the Wind • Endless Love • In the Still of the Night • Just the Way You Are • Memory • The Nearness of You • People • The Rainbow Connection • Smile • Unchained Melody • What a Wonderful World • Yesterday • and more.
00117051 . . . . $24.99

PETER, PAUL & MARY

Over 40 songs: And When I Die • Blowin' in the Wind • Goodnight Irene • If I Had a Hammer (The Hammer Song) • Leaving on a Jet Plane • Puff the Magic Dragon • This Land Is Your Land • We Shall Overcome • Where Have All the Flowers Gone? • and more.
00121822 . . . . $14.99

THREE CHORD SONGS

60 songs: Bad Case of Loving You • Bang a Gong (Get It On) • Blue Suede Shoes • Cecilia • Get Back • Hound Dog • Kiss • Me and Bobby McGee • Not Fade Away • Rock This Town • Sweet Home Chicago • Twist and Shout • You Are My Sunshine • and more.
00702483 . . . . $15.99

TOP HITS

31 hits: The A Team • Born This Way • Forget You • Ho Hey • Jar of Hearts • Little Talks • Need You Now • Rolling in the Deep • Teenage Dream • Titanium • We Are Never Ever Getting Back Together • and more.
00115929 . . . . $14.99

Prices, contents, and availability subject to change without notice.

HAL•LEONARD®

www.halleonard.com

0722
238